AF584847

For Andy and our beautiful girl.
Grow true xo

Scholastic Press
An imprint of Scholastic Australia Pty Limited
PO Box 579 Gosford NSW 2250
ABN 11 000 614 577
www.scholastic.com.au

Part of the Scholastic Group
Sydney · Auckland · New York · Toronto · London · Mexico City
New Delhi · Hong Kong · Buenos Aires · Puerto Rico

Published by Scholastic Australia in 2026.

A catalogue record for this book is available from the National Library of Australia

ISBN: 978-1-76172-381-0 (hardback)

Ben Knight created these illustrations digitally.
Typeset in Avera Sans TC.
Book design by Nicole Stofberg.

Printed in China by RR Donnelley.
Scholastic Australia's policy, in association with RR Donnelley, is to use papers that are renewable and made efficiently from wood grown in responsibly managed sources, so as to minimise its environmental footprint.

10 9 8 7 6 5 4 3 2 1 26 27 28 29 30 / 2

WOWEE! LOOK AT THAT TREE!

BEN KNIGHT

A Scholastic Press book from Scholastic Australia

I'm not really sure why I'm me.
Why have I grown into a tree?
Why not a bird? Why not a bee?
I guess I'll just have to be me.

I'm only tiny, but I know
a good tree always has to grow.
But why straight up? Why is it so?
I'm in charge of how I grow.

So, I do, with all my might.
I grow myself off to the right.
Trees my age laugh at the sight,
teasing me about my height.

'WOWEE!

Look at that TREE!'

The other saplings laugh at me.

'It's crooked, bent and so unusual.
This tree is weird and so **delusional!**'

The seasons change,
the wind, it blows . . .

but to the side
I grow and grow.

My leaves turn red,
then fall below.

I grow through sun,
through rain and snow.

But then I hear from way up high,
the big, old trees look down and sigh.
A good tree should grow to the sky.
From up above I hear them cry . . .

'WOWEE!
Look at that
TREE!'

The elders all point down at me.
'It's crooked, bent and so unusual.

This tree is weird and so **confusable!'**

Now, strange creatures run around quick,
giving all the trees a big red tick.
They walk up to me. Will I get picked?
One of them gives my trunk a kick . . .

'WOWEE!

Look at that TREE!'

The creatures all look up at me.

'It's crooked, bent and so unusual.
This tree is weird. It is **unusable!**'

Now other things grow near me,
but they don't look quite like a tree.
They are as tall as can be.
My new friends? I'll wait and see.

But when I say hi, they don't reply.

Is it me? I don't know why.

My tree tears well; I start to cry.

But then I hear a voice . . .

'Hey, guys!'

'WOWEE!

Look at that TREE!'

A tiny creature looks up at me.

'It's crooked, bent and so unusual . . .

. . . this tree is
PERFECT!

This tree is BEAUTIFUL!’

My tree tears well again, but now
it's happy tears that trickle down.
What is this feeling that I've found?
There's joy and laughter all around.

So, if you're down, please don't be blue.
Not everyone will love what you do.
There might be a million, or only two . . .
but someone will always love you for you.

Wowea